When I Baptized

A Fun LDS Coloring book for kids

By Ed Gonzalez

for my son Robbie.

I will follow Jesus.

I will make my parents happy.

I will invite family and friends.

I will promise to be good.

I will have prayers offered.

I will have talks given.

I will dress in white clothing.

I will have pictures taken.

People will remember their baptisms.

I will be baptized by authority.

I will have my sins forgiven.

I will get the gift of the Holy Ghost.

I will sing songs.

The Bishop will welcome me.

I will have refreshments.

I will get lots of hugs.

I will become a member
of the Church of Jesus Christ.

I will show God I love him.

I will take the sacrament purposefully.

I will be an example to others.

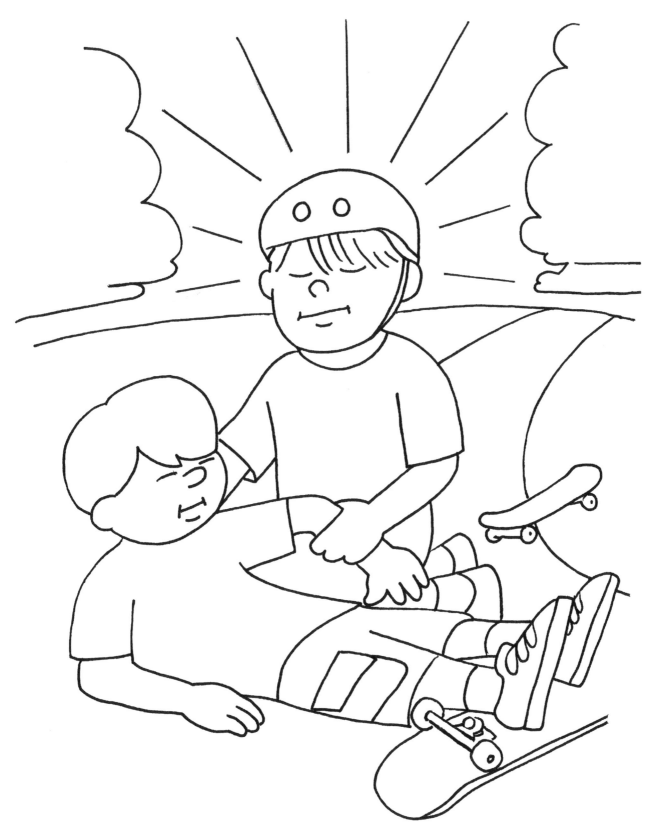

I will be a disciple of Jesus Christ.

I will always remember my baptism.

I will be so happy.

I will be able to return to
my Father in Heaven someday.

Jesus was baptized.

Jesus answered, Verily, verily I say
unto thee, Except a man be born of water and
of the spirit, he cannot enter into the
Kingdom of God.   (John 3:5)

We believe in God, the Eternal Father,
and in His Son, Jesus Christ,
and in the Holy Ghost.

We believe that men will be
punished for their own sins, and
not for Adam's transgression.

We believe that through the Atonement of Christ, all mankind may be saved, by obedience to the laws and ordinances of the Gospel.

HOLY GHOST

BAPTISM

REPENTANCE

FAITH

We believe that the first principles and ordinances of the Gospel are:
first, Faith in the Lord Jesus Christ; second, Repentance;
third, Baptism by immersion for the remission of sins;
fourth, Laying on of hands for the gift of the Holy Ghost.

We believe that a man must be called of God, by prophecy, and by the laying on of hands by those who are in authority, to preach the Gospel and administer in the ordinances thereof.

We believe in the same organization
that existed in the Primitive Church, namely,
apostles, prophets, pastors, teachers,
evangelists, and so forth.

We believe in the gift of tongues,
prophecy, revelation, visions, healing,
interpretation of tongues, and so forth.

We believe the Bible to be the word of God
as far as it is translated correctly;
we also believe the Book of Mormon
to be the word of God.

We believe all that God has revealed, all that He does now reveal, and we believe that He will yet reveal many great and important things pertaining to the Kingdom of God.

We believe in the literal gathering of Israel and in the restoration of the Ten Tribes; that Zion (the New Jerusalem) will be built upon the American continent; that Christ will reign personally upon the earth; and, that the earth will be renewed and receive its paradisiacal glory.

We claim the privilege of worshiping Almighty God
according to the dictates of our own conscience,
and allow all men the same privilege, let them
worship how, where, or what they may.

We believe in being subject to kings,
presidents, rulers, and magistrates,
in obeying, honoring, and sustaining the law.

We believe in being honest, true, chaste, benevolent, virtuous, and in doing good to all men; indeed, we may say that we follow the admonition of Paul-We believe all things, we hope all things, we have endured many things, and hope to be able to endure all things. If there is anything virtuous, lovely, or of good report or praiseworthy, we seek after these things.

Jesus saith I am the way,
the truth, and the life, no man
cometh unto the Father,
but by me. (John 14:6)

When I am Baptized

Published by Ed Gonzalez
© Copyright 2011
All rights reserved

Made in the U.S.A.

Proof

Made in the USA
Charleston, SC
11 September 2011